CURSIVE HANDWRITING

WORKBOOK

for Children

Copyright:

All content within this "Cursive Handwriting Workbook for Children", including texts, templates, and designs, is protected by copyright. The intellectual property rights belong to us and may not be reproduced, duplicated, or used in any form without our explicit permission.

Disclaimer:

The information and guidance provided in this workbook are for general purposes only. We make no representations or warranties of any kind, express or implied, about the completeness, accuracy, reliability, suitability, or availability of the information contained herein. Any reliance you place on such information is therefore strictly at your own risk.

While we strive to provide accurate and up-to-date content, we do not guarantee the accuracy or effectiveness of the techniques, strategies, or advice presented in this workbook. We shall not be held liable for any errors, omissions, or damages arising from the use of this workbook or the information it contains.

It is important to note that this workbook is not a substitute for professional advice or assistance. If you require specific guidance or have any concerns, we recommend consulting a qualified professional.

By using this "Cursive Handwriting Workbook for Children", you acknowledge and accept the terms of this Copyright & Disclaimer statement.

Table of Contents

Welcome to
Cursive Handwriting!

Welcome to the exciting world of cursive handwriting! This workbook is designed to introduce you to the beautiful and flowing art of cursive writing, which has been a form of communication for centuries. Long before the digital age, people around the world used cursive handwriting to craft personal letters, keep journals, and record important events.

Why Cursive?

Cursive writing is not only about making your handwriting prettier; it's about connecting with history and developing a skill that can improve your fine motor abilities and cognitive skills. As you learn to write in cursive, you'll notice your thoughts flowing as smoothly as your pen on paper!

Did You Know?

Cursive writing was once the standard for all personal and business correspondence!

Why Learn Cursive Writing?

The Benefits of Learning Cursive:

- Improved Writing Speed: Cursive writing allows you to write faster as the pen seldom lifts from the paper.
- Enhanced Motor Skills: Developing cursive writing skills improves hand-eye coordination and fine motor skills.
- Boosted Memory and Learning: Writing in cursive activates areas of the brain involved in thinking, language, and working memory.
- Artistic Expression: Cursive writing is like art; each stroke you make adds beauty and style to your letters.

Setting Up for Success:

- To make the most of your cursive writing practice, it's important to start with the right posture and grip:
- Proper Posture: Sit up straight with your feet flat on the floor. Keep your back straight and shoulders relaxed.
- Correct Grip: Hold your pen or pencil firmly but gently, with your thumb and forefinger grasping the writing instrument and your middle finger supporting it from below.

Tips for Great Practice:

- Take Regular Breaks: Don't tire your hand out. Take a five-minute break every 20 minutes.
- Practice Regularly: Like any skill, regular practice is the key to success.
- Keep Your Paper at a Slight Angle: This makes it easier to write in cursive and helps improve the fluidity of your strokes.

Remember, learning cursive is a journey. Each page in this workbook is a step forward in mastering this beautiful skill. Enjoy every stroke, and let your cursive journey begin!

Letter a - Lowercase

Learn how to write the lowercase 'a'. Start at the top, curve down.

Trace the 'a', then practice writing it freely.

a a a a a a a

a a a a a a a

a a a a a a a

Fun Fact: The letter 'a' looks like a round apple with a tail.

Letter b - Lowercase

Start at the bottom, pull up and loop around for 'b'.

Follow the guide, then try on your own.

Tip: Think of 'b' as a balloon floating up in the sky.

Letter c - Lowercase

Curve around to start 'c', a simple swing.

Trace and then recreate the 'c' without help.

c   c   c   c   c   c   c   c

c   c   c   c   c   c   c   c

c   c   c   c   c   c   c   c

Fun Fact: 'c' is like a crescent moon smiling down at you.

Letter d - Lowercase

Pull up tall and loop down for 'd'.

Practice 'd' with guides, then independently.

d d d d d d d

d d d d d d d

d d d d d d d

Fun Fact: The letter 'd' stands tall like a dinosaur's back.

Letter e - Lowercase

Start in the middle, curl around for 'e'.

Trace, then write 'e' on your own.

e e e e e e e

e e e e e e e

e e e e e e e

Fun Fact: 'e' curls like the tail of a curious cat.

Letter f - Lowercase

Loop up and over to form 'f'.

Follow the fading guides to perfect 'f'.

Fun Fact: 'f' waves like a flag in the wind.

Letter g - Lowercase

Swing around and down below the line for 'g'.

Trace and independently practice 'g'.

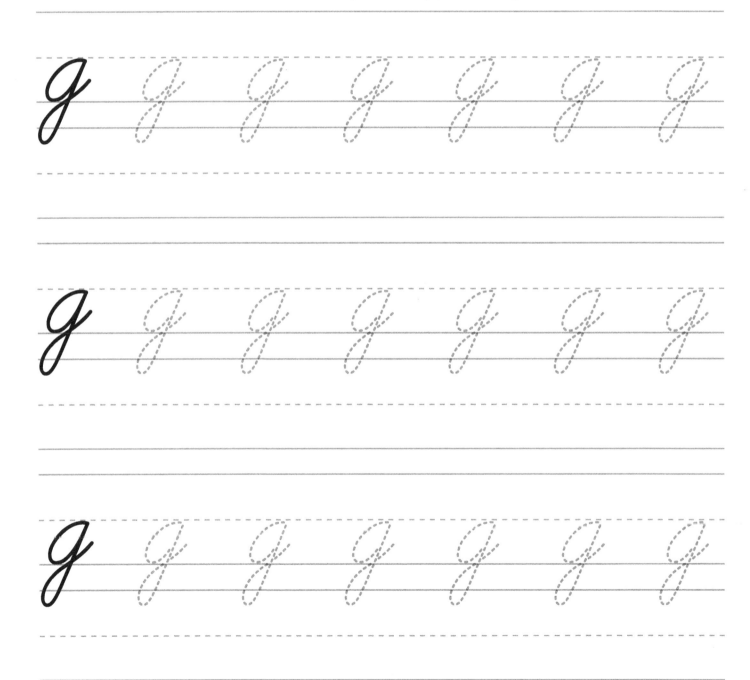

Tip: Think of 'g' as a gumball dropping down from a machine.

Letter h – Lowercase

Pull up, dive down and loop for 'h'.

Guided tracing of 'h', then on your own.

h h h h h h h h h h h

h h h h h h h h h h h

h h h h h h h h h h h

Fun Fact: 'h' hops like a happy rabbit.

Letter i - Lowercase

A simple stroke down, then dot the 'i'.

• 3

Practice 'i' with and without the guide.

Fun Fact: Dotting an 'i' is like popping a balloon gently.

Letter j - Lowercase

Stroke down below the line, then a slight hook and dot for 'j'.

Trace 'j', then practice freely.

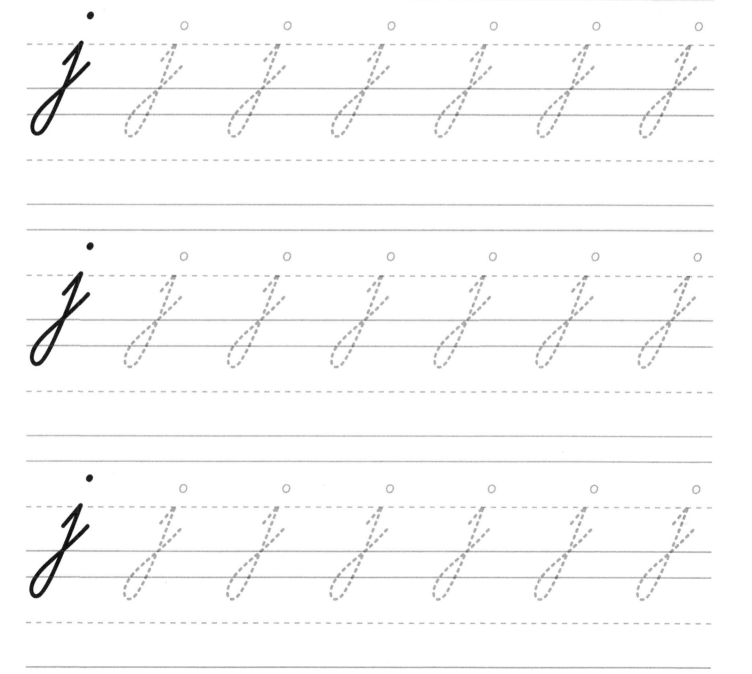

Fun Fact: 'j' jumps down and curls up like a fishhook.

Letter k - Lowercase

Pull up, loop in, and kick out for 'k'.

Guided 'k' practice, then write it alone.

Fun Fact: 'k' kicks like a karate move.

Letter l – Lowercase

A simple upward stroke, curve at the top for 'l'.

Trace 'l', then practice independently.

l l l l l l l

l l l l l l l

l l l l l l l

Fun Fact: 'l' loops like a lemon peel.

Letter m - Lowercase

Start with a curve up, then two humps for 'm'.

Practice 'm' with guides, then by yourself.

m m m m m

m m m m m

m m m m m

Fun Fact: 'm' has mountains that you can climb over.

Letter m - Lowercase

A smaller version of 'm', with one hump.

Follow the trace and write 'n' on your own.

n n   n   n   n   n   n

n n   n   n   n   n   n

n n   n   n   n   n   n

Fun Fact: 'n' is like a rolling wave in the ocean.

Letter o - Lowercase

Circle around smoothly to make an 'o'.

Trace and then freely write 'o'.

Tip: 'o' is like the shape of your open mouth when you say it.

Letter p - Lowercase

Dive down, pull up, and loop around for 'p'.

Guided tracing of 'p', then practice alone.

p p p p p p p

p p p p p p p

p p p p p p p

Tip: 'p' plunges down like a diver.

Letter q - Lowercase

Start like an 'a', but extend the tail below the line for 'q'.

Trace 'q', then write it without help.

Fun Fact: 'q' is a queen with a long flowing robe.

Letter r - Lowercase

Start with a mini loop, then a small kick for 'r'.

Trace and then independently write 'r'.

Fun Fact: 'r' has a ruffle on its skirt.

Letter s - Lowercase

Swing back, curve around for 's'.

Practice 's' with guides, then on your own.

Fun Fact: 's' snakes around like a slithering serpent.

Letter t – Lowercase

Pull up tall, cross over with a flick for 't'.

Guided practice of 't', then free writing.

t t t t t t t

t t t t t t t

t t t t t t t

Tip: 't' stands tall and wears a hat.

Letter u – Lowercase

Dive down, curve up twice for 'u'.

Trace 'u', then practice writing it freely.

u u u u u u u

Fun Fact: 'u' is like a cup that can hold your favorite drink.

26

Letter v - Lowercase

A sharp dip down and up for 'v'.

Practice 'v' with and without the guide.

Tip: 'v' is like a valley between two mountains.

Letter w - Lowercase

Down, up, down again, and up for 'w'.

Guided 'w' practice, then independently.

Fun Fact: 'w' is double 'v' and looks like water waves.

Letter x - Lowercase

Cross in the middle, start and finish high for 'x'.

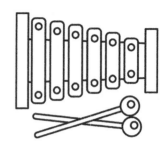

Trace 'x', then write it on your own.

Fun Fact: 'x' marks the spot on a treasure map.

Letter y - Lowercase

Down, loop, and long tail below the line for 'y'.

Practice 'y' with guides, then alone.

Fun Fact: 'y' yawns down and dips below like a yo-yo.

Letter z - Lowercase

Zig-zag from top to bottom for 'z'.

Trace 'z', then freehand practice.

Tip: 'z' zips back and forth like a lightning bolt.

Letter A - Uppercase

Learn how to write the uppercase 'A'. Start with a sharp peak.

Trace the 'A', then practice writing it freely.

Fun Fact: The letter 'A' looks like a sharp mountain peak.

Letter B - Uppercase

Begin with a vertical line and add two bubbles for 'B'.

Follow the guide, then try on your own.

B B B B B

B B B B B

B B B B B

Tip: Think of 'B' as a butterfly with two beautiful wings.

Letter C - Uppercase

Create a wide, open curve for 'C'.

Trace and then recreate the 'C' without help.

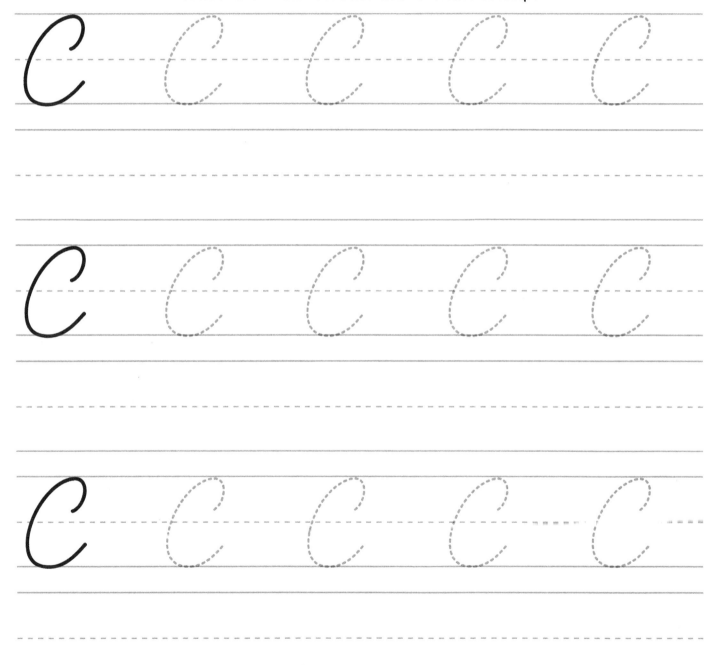

Fun Fact: 'C' is like a crescent moon that's wide open.

Letter D - Uppercase

Start with a straight backbone then add a large, round curve for 'D'.

Practice 'D' with guides, then independently

$\mathcal{D}$ $\mathcal{D}$ $\mathcal{D}$ $\mathcal{D}$ $\mathcal{D}$

$\mathcal{D}$ $\mathcal{D}$ $\mathcal{D}$ $\mathcal{D}$ $\mathcal{D}$

$\mathcal{D}$ $\mathcal{D}$ $\mathcal{D}$ $\mathcal{D}$ $\mathcal{D}$

Tip: The letter 'D' stands tall and round like a drum.

Letter E - Uppercase

Begin with a few sharp, horizontal lines connected by a vertical line.

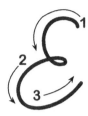

Trace, then write 'E' on your own.

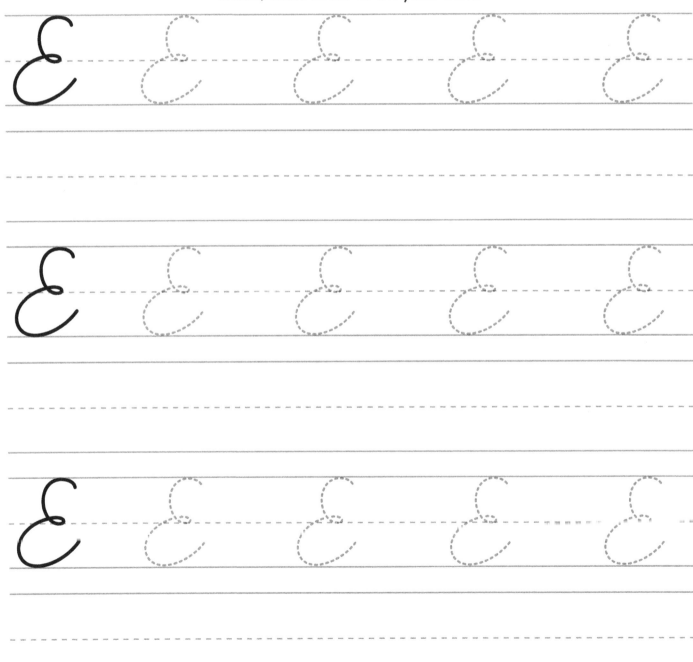

Tip: 'E' has three horizontal bars like a ladder.

Letter F - Uppercase

Start with a long backbone and two crossbars for 'F'.

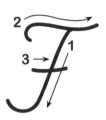

Follow the fading guides to perfect 'F'.

Tip: 'F' is like a flagpole with two flags."

Letter G - Uppercase

Create a 'C' shape, then add a tail to close it for 'G'.

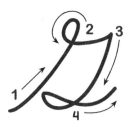

Trace and independently practice 'G'.

Fun Fact: 'G' opens up like a growing plant.

Letter H - Uppercase

Two vertical lines connected by a bridge in the middle for 'H'.

Guided tracing of 'H', then on your own.

Tip: 'H' stands like a bridge between two tall towers.

Letter I - Uppercase

A single line with a stroke at the top and a dot for 'I'.

Practice 'I' with and without the guide.

$\mathcal{I}$ $\mathcal{I}$ $\mathcal{I}$ $\mathcal{I}$ $\mathcal{I}$

$\mathcal{I}$ $\mathcal{I}$ $\mathcal{I}$ $\mathcal{I}$ $\mathcal{I}$

$\mathcal{I}$ $\mathcal{I}$ $\mathcal{I}$ $\mathcal{I}$ $\mathcal{I}$

Fun Fact: Dotting an 'I' is like putting a cherry on top of a sundae.

Letter J - Uppercase

Start high, swoop down below the line and curl slightly for 'J'.

Trace 'J', then practice freely.

J J J J J

J J J J J

J J J J J

Tip: 'J' jumps down and curls up like a fancy hook.

Letter K - Uppercase

Vertical line with two angled strokes coming out for 'K'.

Guided 'K' practice, then write it alone.

K K K K K K K

K K K K K

K K K K K

Fun Fact: 'K' kicks out like a karate chop.

Letter L - Uppercase

A tall, vertical stroke with a base at the bottom for 'L'.

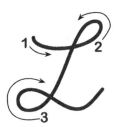 

Trace 'L', then practice independently.

Tip: 'L' is long and lean like a light pole.

Letter M - Uppercase

Start with a vertical line, add two humps across for 'M'.

Practice 'M' with guides, then by yourself.

$\mathcal{M}$ m m m m m m

$\mathcal{M}$ m m m m m m

$\mathcal{M}$ m m m m m m

Fun Fact: 'M' has mountains that reach up high in the sky.

Letter N - Uppercase

One vertical line with a sharp peak across for 'N'.

Follow the trace and write 'N' on your own.

Tip: 'N' nests gently in the middle with a nudge.

Letter O - Uppercase

A full, round shape closing neatly for 'O'.

Trace and then freely write 'O'.

Fun Fact: 'O' circles around like a perfect loop.

Letter P - Uppercase

A tall backbone with a round curve at the top for 'P'.

Guided tracing of 'P', then practice alone.

Tip: 'P' puffs out at the top like a proud chest.

Letter Q - Uppercase

Like an 'O', but with a creative tail swinging out for 'Q'.

Trace 'Q', then write it without help.

Fun Fact: 'Q' is a queen with a quirky tail.

Letter R - Uppercase

Start with a vertical line; add a round top and a kick out for 'R'.

Trace and then independently write 'R'.

Letter S - Uppercase

Begin at the top, curve around tightly for 'S'.

Practice 'S' with guides, then on your own.

Fun Fact: 'S' swirls like a snake sliding through the grass.

Letter T - Uppercase

A tall vertical line crossed near the top for 'T'.

Guided practice of 'T', then free writing.

Tip: 'T' towers tall and is topped with a hat.

Letter U - Uppercase

Start low, scoop up, and return smoothly for 'U'.

Trace 'U', then practice writing it freely.

$\mathcal{U}$ $\mathcal{U}$ $\mathcal{U}$ $\mathcal{U}$ $\mathcal{U}$

$\mathcal{U}$ $\mathcal{U}$ $\mathcal{U}$ $\mathcal{U}$ $\mathcal{U}$

$\mathcal{U}$ $\mathcal{U}$ $\mathcal{U}$ $\mathcal{U}$ $\mathcal{U}$

Fun Fact: 'U' is like a cup holding up the universe.

Letter V - Uppercase

Start high, plunge down sharply, and rise again for V'.

Practice V' with and without the guide.

V   V   V   V   V   V

V   V   V   V   V   V

V   V   V   V   V   V

Tip: V' vanishes into a valley and vaults back out.

Letter W - Uppercase

Like 'V', but doubled—down, up, down again, and up for 'W'.

Guided 'W' practice, then independently.

Fun Fact: 'W' waves twice, like a double cheer.

Letter X - Uppercase

Cross two lines in the middle crisply for 'X'.

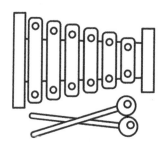

Trace 'X', then write it on your own.

Tip: 'X' marks the spot on ancient treasure maps.

Letter Y - Uppercase

A 'V' with a long tail dropping below the line for 'Y'.

Practice 'Y' with guides, then alone.

Fun Fact: 'Y' yawns down and sptretches out like a yo-yo.

Letter Z - Uppercase

Start at the top, zigzag sharply and finish with a horizontal line for 'Z'.

Trace 'Z', then freehand practice.

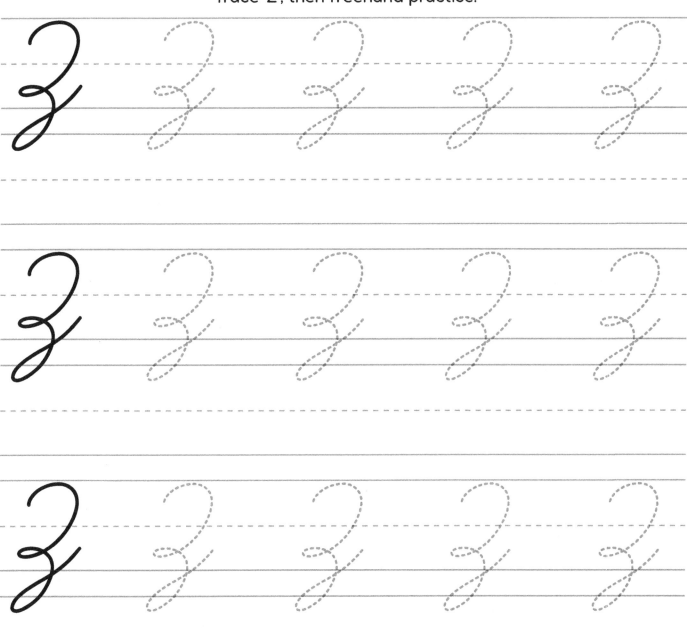

Tip: 'Z' zips across quickly like a lightning strike.

Letter Connections - a to t

Learn to connect 'a' to 't'. Common in words like 'cat' and 'hat'.

Trace the connection, then practice without guides.

at   *at*   *at*   *at*   *at*

at   *at*   *at*   *at*   *at*

cat   *hat*   *mat*

Keep your connections smooth for beautiful cursive writing!

Letter Connections - e to l

Connecting 'e' to 'l' often appears in words such as 'bell' and 'tell'.

Guided practice fading to independent writing.

el   *el*   *el*   *el*   *el*

el   *el*   *el*   *el*   *el*

bell   *tell*   *well*

Practice makes perfect—keep going!

Letter Connections - i to n

Practice connecting 'i' to 'n', used in 'win' and 'pin'.

Start with tracing, move to freehand practice.

in   *in*   *in*   *in*   *in*

in   *in*   *in*   *in*   *in*

win   *thin*   *pin*

Each stroke brings you closer to cursive mastery!

Letter Connections - o to v

o' to 'v' transition is key for words like 'over' and 'novel'.

Trace and then write on your own using the lines provided.

ov   ov   ov   ov   ov

ov   ov   ov   ov   ov

over   novel

Your cursive is getting smoother!

Letter Connections - s to a

The connection from 's' to 'a' can be seen in 'sack' and 'ask'.

Practice with guides, then independently.

sa   *sa*   *sa*   *sa*   *sa*

sa   *sa*   *sa*   *sa*   *sa*

sack   *ask*   *mask*

Great job! Keep connecting those letters!

Letter Connections - r to e

Connecting 'r' to 'e' is found in words like 'tree' and 'free'.

Begin with tracing exercises, then freely write.

re   *re*   *re*   *re*   *re*

re   *re*   *re*   *re*   *re*

tree   *free*   *agree*

Your hard work is showing in your handwriting!

Letter Connections - n to d

'n' to 'd' appears in words like 'and' 'land' and 'sand'.

Guided to independent practice on the lines.

nd nd nd nd nd

nd nd nd nd nd

and land sand

Letter Connections - c to h

Learn the smooth transition from 'c' to 'h' in words like 'chance' and 'arch'.

Trace, then practice the connection freely.

ch ch ch ch ch ch ch ch

ch ch ch ch ch ch ch ch

chance *arch*

You're doing fantastic with your cursive connections!

Letter Connections - m to o

Master connecting 'm' to 'o' in words such as 'mood' and 'moon'.

Trace fading guides, then write without assistance.

mo *mo mo mo*

mo *mo mo mo*

mood moon

Letter Connections - b to y

Practice the unique connection from 'b' to 'y' found in 'by' and 'baby'.

Start with guided lines, progress to freehand practice.

by   *by*   *by*   *by*

by   *by*   *by*   *by*

by baby maybe

Your cursive will soon be flawless!

Sight Words and Simple Sentences

Trace each word, then write them independently.

the   and   to   you   it

the   and   to   you   it

The cat ran to you.

You see it.

Sight Words and Simple Sentences

Guided tracing for each word, followed by freehand practice.

he was for on are

he was for on are

He was on the mat.

Are they here?

Amazing effort! These words are your reading helpers!

Sight Words and Simple Sentences

Trace words; attempt forming them without guides after.

as with his they I

the and to you it

I play with my toys.

His dog is big.

Sight Words and Simple Sentences

Practice tracing and then writing each word on your own.

at be this have from

at be this have from

Have fun at the park.

Be kind to others.

Keep practicing for even smoother writing!

Sight Words and Simple Sentences

Trace, then recreate the words freely to gain confidence.

or one had by words

or one had by words

She had one wish.

Buy words for learning.

Your hard work is showing in your handwriting!

Sight Words and Simple Sentences

Begin with guided exercises, then write independently.

but not what all were

but not what all were

All were happy.

What is that?

You're making great progress!

Sight Words and Simple Sentences

Trace the words, then practice writing them in cursive independently.

we when your can said

we when your can said

We said goodbye.

Can your mom come?

Keep up the great work!

Sight Words and Simple Sentences

Guided practice fading to independent writing.

there use an each which

there use an each which

Use the door.

Which one is yours?

Your cursive is getting smoother!

Sight Words and Simple Sentences

Trace fading guides, then write without assistance.

how their if will up

how their if will up

How will they go up?

Their house is big.

Sight Words and Simple Sentences

Start with guided lines, progress to freehand practice.

about out many then them

about out many then them

Many of them laughed.

Then, they went out.

Your cursive will soon be flawless!

Inspirational Quotes & Phrases

Trace the phrase, then write it freely to express yourself.

Believe in yourself

Believe in yourself

Believe in yourself

Believe in yourself

Dream big, work hard

Dream big, work hard

Dream big, work hard

Dream big, work hard

Great effort leads to great achievements!

Inspirational Quotes & Phrases

Start with tracing, move to writing it on your own.

Every day is a new beginning

Every day is a new beginning

Every day is a new beginning

Every day is a new beginning

Embrace each new day with a fresh start in your writing!

Inspirational Quotes & Phrases

Guided practice, then freehand expression.

Kindness is wisdom

Kindness is wisdom

Kindness is wisdom

Kindness is wisdom

Kind words can change the world. Keep practicing!

Inspirational Quotes & Phrases

Trace first, then write with your personal flair.

Follow your heart

Follow your heart

Follow your heart

Follow your heart

Let your cursive flow as freely as your dreams!

Inspirational Quotes & Phrases

Practice the phrase with guidance, then on your own.

Stay curious, keep learning

Stay curious, keep learning

Stay curious, keep learning

Stay curious, keep learning

Curiosity leads to discovery. Write on!

Trace the phrase, then try to write it smoothly on your own.

Patience brings rewards

Patience brings rewards

Patience brings rewards

Patience brings rewards

Patience in practice makes perfect.

Laughter is timeless

Laughter is timeless

Laughter is timeless

Laughter is timeless

Fill your pages and your life with joy!

Inspirational Quotes & Phrases

Trace and then recreate the phrase freely.

Be brave, take risks

Be brave, take risks

Be brave, take risks

Be brave, take risks

Courage in writing reflects courage in life!

Inspirational Quotes & Phrases

Start with guided lines, progress to freehand.

Create your own sunshine

Create your own sunshine

Create your own sunshine

Create your own sunshine

Your bright words light up the page!

Cursive Art

Trace 'Butterfly' in cursive, then write it on your own.

Butterfly   *Butterfly*

You're making your cursive as beautiful as art!

Cursive Art

Practice tracing 'Sunshine' in cursive, followed by freehand.

Brighten your page with lovely cursive writing!

Cursive Art

Trace the word 'Tree', then recreate it in your style.

Tree Tree Tree Tree

Your words grow strong like a tree!

Cursive Art

Guided cursive practice for 'Ocean', then independent writing.

Let your cursive flow like ocean waves!

Cursive Art

Trace 'Castle' in cursive and then try writing it freely.

Build your cursive skills as tall as a castle!

Progress Checkpoint

Write the cursive letters **A to M** from memory.
Try to recall the correct form and spacing.

Amazing progress! Let's keep refining those letters!

Progress Checkpoint

Complete the alphabet by writing letters **N to Z** in cursive.
Focus on smooth connections.

You're doing great! Every letter you write is improving.

Progress Checkpoint

Revisit the letter pairs **th, ch, st**.
Write them and try to connect them smoothly.

th   th   ch   ch   st   st

Your connections are getting smoother! Keep practicing!

Progress Checkpoint

Write the sentence '**The quick brown fox jumps over the lazy dog**'
to use every letter.

The quick brown fox jumps

over the lazy dog

Look how beautifully you've written this! What improvement!

CERTIFICATE
OF COMPLETION

This certifies that

_____

has successfully completed the

Cursive Handwriting Workbook

and demonstrated great skill in cursive writing.

_____

INSTRUCTOR'S SIGNATURE

_____

DATE

Extra Practice Sheets

Made in the USA
Coppell, TX
30 September 2024

37918213R00057